Firebrand

& other poems from my diary

Arya Adake

D1713044

We don't read and write poetry because it's cute. We read and write poetry because we are members of the human race.

And the human race is filled with passion.

- *Robin Williams as John Keating, in Dead Poets Society*

Foreword
In Light of Recent Events

A few months ago, the current situation we are in with the COVID-19 pandemic would have been unthinkable. When school closed for the rest of the year, the first weeks were a much-needed way to unwind, and even a gift. But now, the loneliness and boredom have started to set in. We, as students, try to keep it at bay with exciting new discoveries. Rediscovering our passions. We have written ourselves into frenzies, sketched and painted our way into the light, baked and sung and practiced the sadness away.

But we see the climbing figures and the same four walls every day, and suddenly poems are just words on a page. Paintings are flashes of lines and colors. Even our carefully curated new discoveries start to look the same.

To prevent that from happening, I've decided to write down how I feel; words have always been a beautiful medium for me to express myself, and I need them now more than ever.

I hope that by reading these poems, you find some comfort or a little bit of happiness!

And be on the lookout for more of these, because we're in for a long haul.

Welcome to "Firebrand."

Dedication

Mrs. Steinberg, this is for you... for your dedication and unwavering positivity, and for planting the seed in my mind that eventually bloomed into this book.

To you, for your undying love for literature, education, and kids.

To you, especially for how you made new worlds come alive for me.

I love you, and I am so, so grateful for you!

Acknowledgments

To my parents, whose constant encouragement and support spanned the chasm between knowing I could do this and believing I could.

To my family, especially my amazing, lovable cousins, who make me the luckiest girl alive and always make me feel special. I love you so much!

To Shivani, for being the best friend I could possibly have, for making me laugh, giving it to me straight, and standing by me even when I didn't make it easy.

To Arvind Kaka, Gautami Tai, and Abha, for the gorgeous illustrations that pull this book together, and for being so helpful and open to suggestions. I am so grateful for all of you!

To everyone who has ever supported or believed in my writing – *Your words made the difference.*

Diary Entries

C. Nature   45

D. Hope   57

Poetry and Me

Writing this, my first instinct is to glorify poetry, to launch into heartfelt explanations of how much it means to me. But I've read enough impassioned introductions to know that if you haven't already skipped over this, a tirade of *"poetry is so beautiful"* will push you right over the edge into *"all right, enough already"* territory. So I'm not going to explain how much writing poetry means to me. I'm just going to tell you a story.

On my sixth birthday, my parents gave me 4 books. I loved to read, so naturally I was excited - until I flipped through one of them. It was Wordsworth and Shakespeare, full of long words and winding epiphanies that meant nothing to me. My vocabulary was pretty much limited to skinny chapter books from the library, so the subtle wordplay and eloquent imagery went so far over my head that even the sky was closer. I smiled a gap-toothed grin and put the books away. So Wordsworth and Shakespeare collected dust behind Junie B. Jones and Magic Tree House.

Second grade, however, changed everything. Mrs. Steinberg's classroom was paradise for a book-hungry seven year old, and her enthusiasm for words and poetry spilled over onto me. I had always loved reading, but it wasn't until Mrs. Steinberg that I began to understand writing, and more specifically, poetry. She showed me for the first time that writing held power, and with words anything could be done. That was around the time I started writing birthday poems. To my parents, to my family and friends. They were usually four lines long in crude handwriting, but my parents stuck them on the fridge all the same, so I kept writing them.

The next revelation came a few years later, the summer before fifth grade. I was in my grandfather, Sanat Dada's, study in India with my knees pulled to my chest and my eyes fixed on the TV. Robin Williams crouched between rows of desks quoting Walt Whitman, and his quiet voice was the loudest sound in the room, even louder than my pounding heart. His speech was like nothing I'd seen before, and long after the credits of *Dead Poets Society* had ended I sat in awestruck silence. It felt like his words were for me, and I fell asleep with them swirling in my head and buzzing in my fingers. I saw myself in Charlie's smirk, in Neil's eyes bright with hope, in Mr. Keating's barely restrained love for poetry. There is nothing quite like the magic of seeing that movie for the first time, being ten years old and feeling something click into place inside, knowing another part of yourself is awake.

As I got older, poetry became a way to explore not only the world around me, but the world within. My poems were vents, affirmations, emotion in the rawest form. They shifted from grandiose delusions of love and life to simple, personal triumphs and tragedies. They moved from airy lines of whimsy and wonder to gritty, sometimes painful truths and trials. They became more personal, and more powerful for it.

Okay, before you point it out, I realize that I just launched into a glorification of poetry - oops.

But honestly, I don't know who I would be without poetry. I hope that over the next few pages, you can see who I am because of it. And who knows, maybe you'll see a little bit of yourself, too.

14

Picture above is from family album / Spring 2018

A.   Love

I have always been in love with the idea of love. When I was little, I adored tales of extravagant romance and splendor. As I grew up, I read countless YA romances and dreamed of love stories written in the stars. I admire my parents' relationship and hope to find a love like theirs someday.

But I recognize, too, that love is extremely complicated, and that not all love stories can have a happy ending. The following poems are my attempt to understand love & the emotions surrounding it.

Enjoy!

1. Paper Boats

Trying to write about you is like trying to hold the night sky.

Fistfuls of inky velvet in each hand, swimming in it, but knowing there's still more up above that ripples when I touch it and that any amount of wanting more will always be inadequate.

Illustration above is from Gautami Khatavkar / April 2020

I have no pretty metaphors about your eyes, no alliterative witticisms about the way you make me feel, no charming quatrains about you and I.
And I've tried, but everything I write comes out like paper boats in a flood,
Flimsy and fleeting.

It's strange but you are the first feeling I can't compress into ink or box into pixels on a screen,
The first feeling I can't speak or write but just know.

How do you do that? I wonder as I smile at an empty page,
How do you take the river of words in my mind and turn it to shy glances, dazzling smiles, the warmth of our hands brushing under the table?

You steal my muse the way you steal my breath,
Tug at the tapestries of words in my head,
Unravel me with a glance and put me back together again.

Trying to write about you is like trying to hold the night sky so just know
That every "I love you" is everything
I don't know how to say.

2. The Way Music Does

He makes me dance the way music does,
Hands and feet as light as air, as light as my heart,
I could wear the stars in my hair and the moon at
my throat.

He makes me laugh the way music does,
Bright and colorful, breathless, a little giddy,
I could lose myself forever in those beautiful eyes.

He makes me think the way music does,
Of the random chance of it all, of the
unbelievable gift we have been given in each
other,
I could write our story in shimmering moonlight
across the sky.

He makes me live the way music does,
Freely, proudly, impossibly bright against the dark,
I could crumble into stardust and he would love
me still.

3. When Poetry Is Inadequate

I wanted to write you a poem,
A page full of my heart,
A lovely, precious, moving thing
That touched you from the start.

I wanted to make you feel special
With sonnets that flowed with ease,
Lines of sweet magic that made you smile
And made you think of me.

I wanted to write all about you,
About the stars that brighten your eyes,
About the spring in your every step
And the comfort of your smile.

I wanted to tell you I love you,
Each flaw and each mistake,
That hand in hand we'd face the world,
And that was all it would take.

I wanted to write you a poem,
I wanted to whisper your name,
But then I remembered that I don't need the words,
Because I know you feel the same.

4. Just Before Dawn

Eyes so bright
Glisten wet through the smile on your face
How I know
Your gentle hands, warm on my skin

On a night
When I have no more dreams that I can chase
When I'm feeling the worst I've ever been.

When I cry
Wipe the tears as they fall from my eyes and
Hold me close, let me hear your beating heart

As I try
To remember that still, the sun will rise and
You and I, we will never be apart.

Illustration above is from Abha Adake/ April 2020

5. The Perfect Thief

A thief with pale cheeks and rose petal lips,
Who drank from my river with elegant sips,
Who frolicked for days in my meadows of green,
Who gave me a ring with a soft pearly sheen.

A thief with dark hair and luminous eyes,
Who laughed with abandon and fed me sweet lies,
Who beckoned with glances that enchanted and teased,
Who captured my notice and wouldn't release.

A girl with slim fingers and a voice like a bird,
That soothed like a balm to all who heard,
She quickened my pulse by just standing close,
She hid all her secrets like a gold-dipped rose.

A girl with bright colors, to cover her past,
She beguiled and bewitched this poor soul, alas!
One morning I woke to find not a glimpse,

Of the girl, who had vanished like a fairytale nymph.
Her liquid gold eyes haunted me from the start,
And how cruel, for she's ran off with my heart.

6. To Understand

Illustration above is from Gautami Khatavkar / April 2020

To understand you is to stare into a cold night with no stars and beg for light.

To understand you is to stand amidst a blizzard and fight to see through the snow.

To understand you is to swim with weights tied to my ankles and hope to breathe air.

To understand me is to draw pictures in the sand and watch as the waves wash them away.

To understand me is to look at old photos and drop to your knees because of my smile.

To understand me is to stare at a book until the words lose all meaning and all you see are letters.

To understand us is to let the last candy melt on my tongue and appreciate how some things are meant to fall apart.

To understand us is to curl your hand around empty space and pretend you weren't searching for my hand.

To understand us is to wake up every morning wearing too-heavy rings and wonder if we ever understood at all.

7. Young Love

A breeze stirs the curtains
As I lay on my bed,
Whisks me back to nights of
Me in black, you in red.

We were young then, and reckless,
We were walking on moonlight,
With just a dress and a necklace,
You lit up the dark night.

Ablaze, we were shining,
Bold, without fear,
Your touch was like lightning
When you pulled me near.

I gave you my sorrows,
You let me confide,
Through uncertain tomorrows,
You stood by my side.

You taught me to live hard,
And fight for what I loved,
I still have the index card,
That fell from your glove.

Your hair was so black then,
Your eyes, so blue,
When you speak of "way back when",
I see the young girl in you.

Your heart was so naive then,
Your mind free of pain,
It hurt me to see you
Cry again and again.

But you told me you'd be strong,
If I was by your side,
You said, "I'll be your strength,
And you can be mine."

You brightened my years,
You still do, to this day,
Through smiles and through tears,
This love never fades.

8. You Wear Them Well

Illustration above is from Gautami Khatavkar / April 2020

You wore love like you wear ball gowns,
Sweeping skirts of pink and gold,
Kind words looped your wrists like bracelets
And their glitter made you bold.

You wore heartbreak like an overcoat,
Stormy wool gone wet with tears,
Your boots crunched over shattered dreams
When you tried to outrun your fears.

You wore healing like a cotton dress,
As pure and light as air,
And the laughter you had learned again
Was the flower in your hair.

9. Love in a Snowstorm

Falling snow,
Don't you know,
Oh, just how I feel?
How can I sit, soft and still, if it truly was all real?

Gusty wind,
Pray do tell
The key to my lost heart,
For though he's there,
I feel like we're
A thousand miles apart.
I love the way his eyes light up when I have made him laugh,
I've known him scarce a year but feel like he's my other half.

Clouds of ash,
Thunder's crash,
Feel the fire in my blood!
It can't be quenched, never will, by raindrops or a flood.

Sparkling ice,
Do be nice.
Reveal the truths you know,

Before my dam breaks and I start to talk all in a
flow.
I love the way his midnight hair
Sweeps into those gentle eyes
And I love the way he whispers, "Everything will be
all right."

Swallow-bird,
Haven't you heard,
The pangs of this aching soul?
If he's not mine and I'm not his,
We never will be whole.

Snowdrifts deep,
Do not keep
This lover from delight,
Together, at last, we will be free
To dance into the night.

10.   Icarus

We were laughing with each other, hand in hand, in the rain,
With starry skies in our eyes and fire in our veins,

We were soaring up together, shining spots against the night,
Searching, daring, wanting, faces turned towards the light.

On wings of dreams we flew a little too close to the sun,
Looking back, we saw the warning signs, but never thought to run.

The world was growing dark, but even then we thought we knew,
As if our love could finish what so many had failed to do.

11.   Belief

they ask if i believe in souls
and i answer *i believe in poetry*

they ask if i believe in destiny
and i answer *i believe in hope*

they ask if i believe in heaven
and i answer *i believe in love*

they ask if i believe in miracles
and i answer *i believe in what i see*

but you are different
so when you whisper into my ear like a prayer
do you believe, do you believe, do you believe?
i laugh and say
darling, the only thing i believe in is you

Picture above is from family album / Summer 2017

B.   Turmoil

I love poetry, and writing in general, for its ability to display the full range of human emotion. The following section contains poems I have mostly written in the past year. The common thread between them is that they show the parts of life that aren't beautiful and picture perfect. They show faithlessness, weakness, pain, and fear, because those emotions are just part of the human experience.

I hope that these poems make you think about what people go through in their personal lives and how important is to remember that not every day can be a good day.

1. Firebrand

you reach for me.

    your words draw blood
    and the pain is sharp
    like nothing I have ever known.

in the dark the trees
reach for me too
and their branches sting my face
like icy black fingers.

Illustration above is from Arvind Kelkar / April 2020

but then a spark lights up the midnight-
it's the trees that thrill with fear,
because when they are burnt to ash and
smoke rises in the air,
i will still be here.

each teardrop is a jewel
i wear with pride,
each mark of your hatred on my skin
a battle scar.

i carry my head high- I will not bow,
not to the likes of you,
not when I'm ablaze with the truth,
with the fire in my veins.

you throw me in the forges every day,
yet you cower from the heat.
don't you know I'm made of flames?
don't you know I'll shake the pain?

so bruise me, batter me, burn me,
but know that one day the sun will shine,
that one day I'll blaze so bright you'll close
your eyes and wish you had never hurt me.

2. Black and Purple

you're bored so you pick at a scab on your arm for something to do.

a couple of days later you look down; it has healed.

you have not.

weeks pass by and purple & black dot your arms like filtered photos dot your instagram feed, each one a perfectly crafted lie you spend hours agonizing over.

you take another one, even though your face hurts from smiling and your friends are too loud.

back home you pick at another scab because there is too much to do.

blood wells;
the box of band-aids is empty.

you breathe hard.
black & purple dance beneath your eyelids.

it is early may. but no one at the party asks why you are wearing long sleeves.

3. Fever Dreams

You're born of fever dreams and feathers of fallen angels' wings,

You're made of light and dark and other wild and precious things.

Your skin is sown with moonlit strands, bright fire in your hair,

And when you sing, molten gold flows softly through the air.

Your fingers flit from place to place like quaint and dainty birds,

And someday, I just know you will move mountains with your words.

You are a jewel bright as the dew on summer-morning grass,

But soon you're bound to break, because your heart is made of glass.

For fever dreams are fickle, angels turn and close their eyes,

And even stars in throes of death will plummet from the skies.

4. Clue

Murky water, shadows thrown against the mansion wall,

Crimson carpets, figures in the dark and empty hall,

Eyes like diamonds, hard and cold that glimmer in the night,

Rubies, snake eyes at her throat that glitter when they catch the light.

Stains of candlewax, still hot, their dripping wet and loud,

Rumors pulse and throb, their whispers heavy in the crowd.

Laughter, fake and bright, to hide the fear that we all smell,

It reeks and makes us shiver as we pretend that all is well.

A scream, a thud, a gasp, a flash of red, and someone's dead,

The wary looks and murmurs say it's getting to our heads.

My palms are sweaty, throat is dry, suspicions wild and thick,

It's her, I say, triumphant, in the sunroom, with the candlestick.

5. Knight

When swallows swim and swordfish soar,
When lions squeak and dormice roar,
When the seas scream beastly battle cries,
The Silver Knight comes from the sky.

When fires shiver and snowfalls burn,
When canyons tremble and oceans churn,
When his sword slides from its gleaming sheath,
The Silver Knight bares gleaming teeth.

When rivers dry and deserts flood,
When the clouds rain down tears and blood,
When lightning sears the sky in half,
The Silver Knight begins to laugh.

When mountains crumble and forests crash,
When flowers turn to dust and ash,
When he sheaths his sword with a black-gloved
hand,
The Silver Knight leaves a shattered land.

6. Sun & Moon

As red as sun in streams of grief it flows,
While overhead the gentle moonlight glows,
A canopy of shining stars provide,
Final relief to souls of those who died.
Lying amidst the cold and trampled snow,
While ice creeps up and frigid winds, they blow,
Their eyes, unseeing, bodies blue from cold,
The shells of people strong and brave and bold.

7. Devour

There's a hunger within me, shaking and thrashing
against my ribs, ardent and bleak.
There's a darkness within me, spilling from my eyes
and dripping from my mouth when I open it to
speak.
There's something wrong within me, so I crack the
bones inscribed with poetry and take to the sky.
There's something wrong within me, so I scream
until dark bleeds into red and fly.

And there's something so magical about the way
silver and black glimmer under my eyelids when I
blink.
The way the stars taste, smoky and electric,
The way the blackness cringes from the stardust on
my hands.
The way yellow lightning burns through me when I
stand.

There's something powerful about the way I land
hard on my knees,
The way the whispered rumors of my midnight
snack are woven through the breeze.
And my belly is full with warmth the way coffee
can never make it,
And I curl up on the ground to sleep, content to
watch an empty sky and not break it.

44

Picture above is from family album / Spring 2017

C. Nature

I believe there are certain things that even words cannot touch, certain things that are so indescribable that marks on a page can never fully capture their meaning. And nature is one of these few and far between things. There's something about the sky at sunset, or the roar of a waterfall, that defies all human understanding.

Nevertheless, nature is one of the most inspiring subjects for me to write about. I hope that by reading the next few poems, you feel a little closer to nature and remember how beautiful it can be.

1. Touches of Twilight

Brilliant colors
Sweet scented air,
Flowers braided,
Through my hair.

    Sky like sapphires,
    Gentle breeze,
    Singing birds,
    Shade of trees.

Picture above is from family album / Winter 2016

Foamy waves
A steady beat,
Water's cool
At my feet.

The sun, a jewel
That sinks beneath
The water's edge
To gently sleep.

Soon the moon
Will sweep the night
Away on wings
Of silver light.

The world will sleep,
Quietly recede,
Into hollows and homes,
But never I-

I'll stay up late,
My eyes as bright
As the sun or moon
Or any light.

2. Spring

Illustration above is from Gautami Khatavkar / April 2020

Chalk smears are fairy dust in the warm April sun,
Dewdrops are diamonds in fields full of fun,

Bubbles are portals to rose-tinted worlds,
And flowers hold dreams in their sweet-scented whorls.

Light as a feather, I'll float on a breeze,
And soar with pink petals from young cherry trees,

Fall asleep on a bed made of clouds with a sigh,
And watch as the robins and swallows fly by.

All the magic of springtime I'll rush to behold,
As sunsets paint cities in shimmering gold.

3. Faerie

As the rain tapers off they awaken at last,
Stretch their legs and clamber out of holes in the trees.
They fall from the sky and burst from the ground,
And millions of them fly, carried by a breeze.

In the wake of the storm, they open their eyes,
Their voices are whispers that sigh with delight,
Come out with the stars and stand perfectly still, for
You might get to meet one tonight.

Remember to bow, for they like that, it seems,
And take care not to step on their feet,
And heed all the things that they tell you,
For such things I may never repeat.

Laugh with abandon, dance with the stars,
And soar on the wings of the sky,
But remember the secrets that they try to hide,
And most of all, remember why.

Don't eat what they offer, don't drink what they give,

In the dark of the moor or the glen,

For if you do, in the morning, you'll be one of them,

Trapped till the rain comes again.

4. The Garden

when i was young i built
a garden in my mind,
all mine,
filled with the plants i needed
even when i didn't know why.

sweet-smelling rosebushes in
everlasting pinks and reds,
in my head,
blooming through rain and snow
even when i couldn't.

pungent bushels of mint and bay leaves like
the smell of home
if i was alone,
wrapping me in familiarity and peace
even when i was homesick.

strawberries and blackberries, plump and bright,
the taste of fun
if i needed one,
exploding in my mouth and bringing sunshine
even when it was dark outside.

when i was young i built
a garden in my mind,
all mine,
and planted in it all the seeds of me,
for when i needed them.

53

5. Stardust

i am the pearly sheen that all your dreams are
glazed with
the frozen beauty of a starry sky
the impossible magic of fireflies on a summer night

i am the flutter of your heart in your throat
the tango of butterflies in your stomach
the pretty pain that splinters through your skin
when you fall

i am the glow of neon lights in the dark
the first splash of paint across an empty canvas
held together by woven words and music

i am the glimmer of sunlight on morning dew
the shimmer of rain on a road
The twinkle of wind chimes in the breeze

i am exploding planets, collapsing worlds
the final sigh before it all goes up in flames
and when the world ends?

i am the stardust left behind

56

Picture above is from family album / Fall 2019

D.   Hope

Hope kind of speaks for itself. It's one of the most important things in our lives, and I hope - *pun intended* - that these poems remind you that people and circumstances can change, and that no bad thing is forever.

That's the most beautiful thing about tomorrow: tomorrow never dies.

1. Reflections on Fifteen Years

I think of me at five.
Short hair, warm laugh, kind eyes.
Hands stained red and blue with marker ink.

Shoes lighting up the twilight, bright pink, when I
skip after the planes in the sky.
Pain splinters through my skin when I fall, bright twin
stains of blood on my knees.
Sitting in the library on Saturday mornings, lower lip
between teeth, new books piled around me.

Incense, velvety and rich, soaking through my
bones with the warmth of summer nights,
I think of me at five.

I think of me at ten.
Learning to fly, testing my limits, basking in the thrill
of double digits.
Metal-rimmed glasses pale purple, nails bitten,
climbing trees,

Shoes slap on sidewalk when I chase my new
discoveries.
Running till my lungs might burst, standing still
listening to my heart beat.
Sitting in my room, curled up, on Saturday
mornings, lower lip between teeth, as new worlds
surround me.

Melodies, vibrant and deep, soaking through my
bones, I can feel those memories when
I think of me at ten.

I am fifteen.
Putting sleep on the back burner, trying to be a
better person, be a better learner,
Questioning with vigor things I've known my whole
life.

Blinking contacts in, blinking tears out of my eyes.
Low heels click on tiled floors as I seize my dreams.
Doors slamming shut all around me, opening
windows so I can breathe.
Sitting at my desk on Saturday mornings, lower lip
between teeth, the new things I learn astound me.

My own words, vivacious and sharp, soaking
through my bones, I am not alone at

Fifteen.

2. Write

One night you'll be sitting at your desk all alone,
All the lights will be off in your quaint little home.
Your coffee will be cold and your bed still unmade,
And you'll think about memories that refuse to fade.

The lamp will spill pools of warm golden light,
The only warmth that you'll have in the dark, frozen night.
Your heart will be heavy, there'll be no hope in sight,
So you'll pull out a pen and paper to write.

The words will pour - thick, wet, and pungent as ink,
It'll be sadder than you know, and harder than you think.
And that night, that feeling, you won't want it to end,
As you eke out a letter that you'll never send.

It'll stay in your desk, far from sunlight and sight,

Till the day that you think things are finally all right.

They say time heals everything, but you know that's not true,

For nothing heals everything, but writing will do.

Illustration above is from Arvind Kelkar / January 2020

3. The girl in the mirror

Of late I often ponder on the girl I was before,
Who saw the world through sightless eyes and never looked for more.

Who wrapped herself in words so that she's never feel the cold,
Who lived behind a paper shield to pretend that she was bold.

She spoke like she knew everything, and then perhaps she did,
For she'd never known a life beyond the pages where she hid.

Illustration above is from Gautami Khatavkar / April 2020

A mirror meant a battle with the person she could be,
A confrontation with the vision only she could see.

It hurt to see the disappointment lurking in her own eyes,
The whispered, "You could be so much if only you would try."

It was agony to know she was lost but not know where to start,
Trapped inside a starry night and left to face her heart.

She learned to spill her soul onto pages like before,
But in a way that didn't trap her and instead opened a door.

She learned to chase her dreams and speak her truth and even cry,
To grow from her catastrophes and fill a golden sky.

Of late I often ponder on all the people I have been,
And of the girl who broke her limits because she dared to look within.

4. I See God

My mother says *God* in a voice rich with faith
> A voice that believes, despite everything.
> She lights incense in the evenings and as smoke curls through the air
>> I see peace.
>> I think I see God.

My father says *God* into the sweet summer night
> As we talk about everything and nothing under scattered white stars.
> He talks about beauty and humanity and as he looks up at the sky
>> I see wonder.
>> I think I see God.

My friend says *God* with a laugh caught in her throat
> She believes in people, in books, more than heaven or hell.
> She smiles when she reads something she likes and as she turns the page
>> I see hope.
>> I think I see God.

I say *God* with faith and doubt warring inside me

> Because if we all have God within us, why aren't we better?

> If we all have God within us, why do we stumble? Why do we fall?

> I close my eyes and
> I see

>> Curls of incense,
>> star-streaked skies,
>> open books.

> I see

>> Pages full of words,
>> golden ghungroos,
>> roaring waterfalls.

I take a deep breath and as I look into the mirror

> I see courage.

> I see dreams.

> I see love.

And for the first time, in that tear-blurred reflection,
I think I see God.

5. Born to live

Illustration above is from Gautami Khatavkar / April 2020

The heavens burst on the day I was born,
All pouring rain and roiling skies,
And my mother whispered through the storm,
My dear, we're born to die.

But we're born for sun, I now believe,
For faces warmed by dappled beams,
For light that sparkles through the trees,
We're born to live our dreams.

We're born for thoughts that love the dark,
For little things that bring us to tears,
We're born to find our brilliant spark,
We're born to face our fears.

We're born to laugh, and sing, and dance,
To seize the things we're dreaming of,
We're born to marvel at random chance,
We're born to fall in love.

The sky was clear on the day I died,
When I had nothing left to give,
And as I slipped away I smiled
Because we are born to live.

6. You Cannot Divide By Zero

You cannot divide by zero, I am told
Over and over.
You cannot divide by something that was
Never there to begin with.
You cannot take something and break it
Into little pieces of nothing.

They use brightly colored fruit
To explain this.
But instead of red apples I see
Red hearts,
And it is heartening.

You cannot take the thoughts that chase each
other
Half-formed around my head and
Dissolve them into empty space.
You cannot take the words running
Through my veins and
Smother them into nonbeing.
You cannot take the wonder in my eyes when I
see fireworks,

The song of friendship that I hear,
The misshapen parts that make me who I am and
Pretend they are nothing.

You cannot pretend that
I am nothing.
You cannot take something, no matter how small
and fleeting it is,
And wear it down so much it ceases to exist.

You cannot divide by zero, I am told.

And each time I hear it, it is a tiny flare of hope.

7. Star

If you open your window at two and a quarter,
While the moon still reigns queen of the sky,
You'll see a star brighter than all of the rest,
To lead you back home tonight.

Keep your eye on the star and don't look away,
And follow wherever it leads you,
Down paths long-forgotten you'll never see again,
Back to the people that need you.

You'll stop for a drink at a bubbling brook,
And the water will call to your heart,
But you need to keep walking through dark and
through dust,
Before the memories tear you apart.

For good or for bad you must go with the star,
And trust in the things that it knows,
You must swallow your fear and open your eyes,
And follow wherever it goes.

And if, years later, you find yourself wanting
An adventure, well then, my dear young friend,
You have only to open your window at night,
And follow the star once again.

8. Quiet Morning

Midnight, clock strikes
Twelve harsh chimes
The sound made of starlight
I'm wishing away daylight
In here

Ink stained, my brain
Reeling from all the pain
Walking down memory lane
I'm safe from all of life's games
In here

Writing, delighting,
The dark so inviting,
I tell myself I'm fighting
But I know I'm just hiding
In here

Sunrise, a bird flies,
Time to face all my lies
Take back control of my life
Say my goodbyes
To here

9. Dear Diary

We're contemplating how we have become strangers to ourselves

And at that very moment, the clock strikes twelve.

The knot in our throat is still there, but not as tight as it was,

And with every deep, deep breath we take it starts to loosen because

It's a new day.

There are new dreams to face, new mistakes to make.

It's a new day.

We have a brand new day with which to find ourselves again.

Illustration above is from Abha Adake / April 2020

until next time!

Made in the USA
Middletown, DE
29 April 2020